Motorcycles

Kate Riggs

seedlings

CREATIVE EDUCATION • CREATIVE PAPERBACKS

Published by Creative Education and Creative Paperbacks
P.O. Box 227, Mankato, Minnesota 56002
Creative Education and Creative Paperbacks are
imprints of The Creative Company
www.thecreativecompany.us

Design by Ellen Huber
Production by Chelsey Luther
Printed in the United States of America

Photographs by Alamy (MLaoPeople, derek watt), Corbis
(Patrick Bennett), Dreamstime (David Acosta Allely, Aneb,
Neacsu Razvan Chirnoaga, Cristi180884, Jose Gil, Mark
Hewitt, Al-fadzly Shah Mohd Nor, Goce Risteski, Julián
Rovagnati, Sergio Schnitzler, James Steidl), Getty Images
(Jonathan Gawler/Fast Bikes Magazine), iStockphoto
(Rutryin), Shutterstock (efecreata media group, Gustavo
Miguel Fernandes, PRILL, AHMAD FAIZAL YAHYA)

Library of Congress Cataloging-in-Publication Data
Riggs, Kate.
Motorcycles / Kate Riggs.
p. cm. — (Seedlings)
Summary: A kindergarten-level introduction to motorcycles,
covering their speed, drivers, role in transportation, and
such defining features as their engines.
Includes index.
ISBN 978-1-60818-522-1 (hardcover)
ISBN 978-1-62832-122-7 (pbk)
1. Motorcycles—Juvenile literature. I. Title. II. Series:
Seedlings.

TL440.15.R542 2015
629.227'5—dc23   2014000183

CCSS: RI.K.1, 2, 3, 4, 5, 6, 7;
RI.1.1, 2, 3, 4, 5, 6, 7; RF.K.1, 3; RF.1.1

9 8 7 6 5 4 3

TABLE OF CONTENTS

Time to ride!

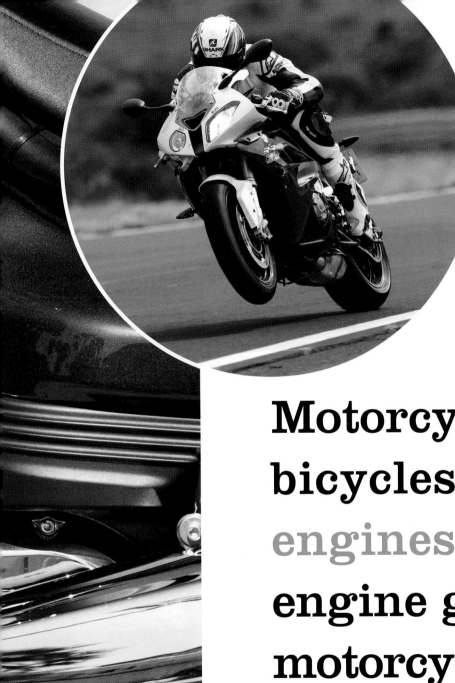

Motorcycles are bicycles with engines. An engine gives a motorcycle power.

Motorcycles have two wheels. The motorcycle **body** is made of metal.

Two handlebars are on top of the body.

A seat is in the middle.

One person drives
a motorcycle.
Sometimes another
person sits behind
the driver.

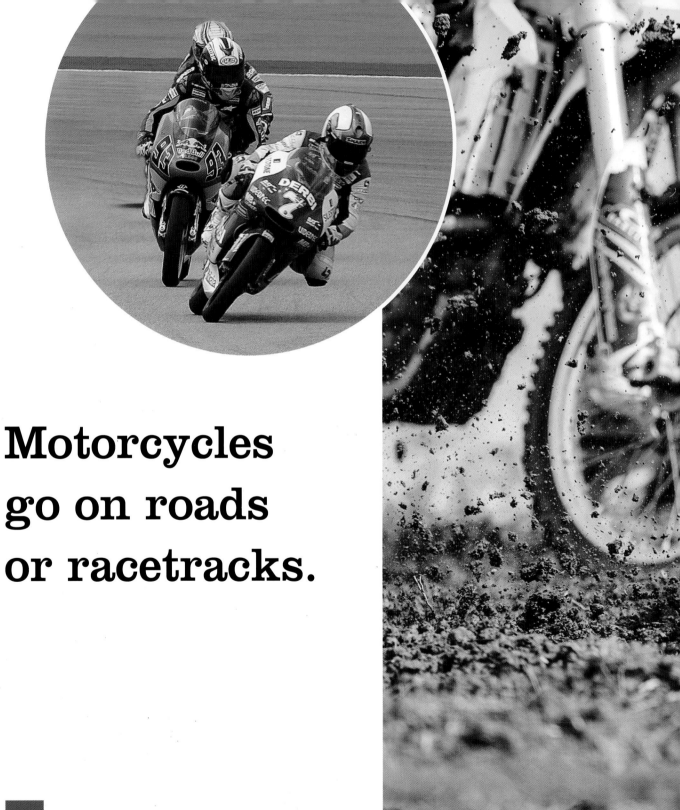

Motorcycles
go on roads
or racetracks.

They can go on dirt, too.

A motorcycle roars down a track. The driver leans in for a curve.

Go,
motorcycle,
go!

Picture a Motorcycle

engine

seat

taillight

turn signal

muffler

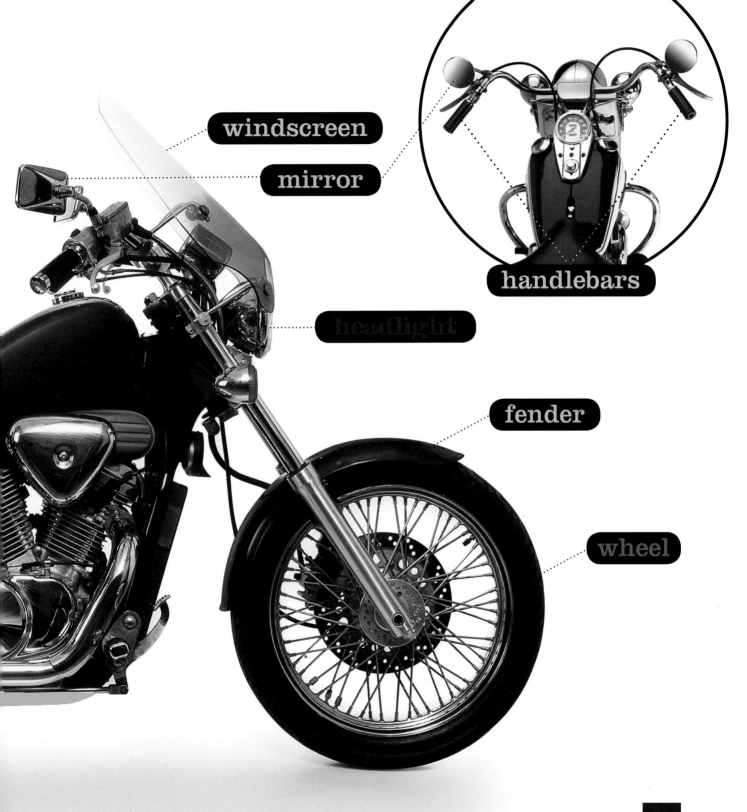

windscreen

mirror

handlebars

headlight

fender

wheel

body: the main part of something

engines: machines inside vehicles that make them move

handlebars: where a motorcycle driver puts his or her hands to make the motorcycle go in the right direction

Read More

Nixon, James. *Motorcycles.*
Mankato, Minn.: Amicus, 2011.

Ridley, Frances. *Amazing Motorcycles.*
Mankato, Minn.: New Forest Press, 2010.

Websites

Motorcycle Coloring Page
http://www.supercoloring.com/pages/motorcycle/
Print out motorcycle pictures to color, or color them online.

Motorcycle Racing Game
http://www.hotwheels.com/en-us/games/motocourse-rally.html
Play a fun motorcycle game!

Index